ADVENTURE

IS

Out there

Published in 2021 by Welbeck Children's Books
An Imprint of Welbeck Children's Limited, part of Welbeck Publishing Group.
20 Mortimer Street London W1T 3JW

Design: Duck Egg Blue Limited
Art Editor: Deborah Vickers

ISBN 978-1-78312-561-6

Printed in Heshan, China
10 9 8 7 6 5 4 3 2 1

A CIP catalogue record for this book is available from the British Library

The publishers would like to thank the following sources for their kind permission to reproduce the pictures in this book.
SHUTTERSTOCK (background and texture elements only):
/Kues 6, 11, 12, 19, 22, 27, 45, 49, 56, 64, 70, 74, 76, 80, 92; /m.rjn 7, 8, 9, 12, 16, 40, 45, 51, 52, 55, 69, 70, 76, 80, 85, 88, 92, 97, 98, 99; /Lena 8, 36, 38, 42, 82, 100; /Monster 10, 13; /Ton Weeyarut Photography 10; /Paladin12 10–11, 18–19; /autsawin uttisin 10, 34, 71, 80, 82; /AnastasiiaM 17; /Sk_Advance studio 22–23, 82–83; /takito 24, 71, /VolodomyrSanych 34, 36, 51, 52, 68, 70, 79, 87, 88, 89; /Lukasz Szwai 60, 98; 78, 86; /Anke Hio 78–79; /Dmitry Fokin 82, 83; /Emqan 88
Every effort has been made to acknowledge correctly and contact the source and/or copyright holder of each picture any unintentional errors or omissions will be corrected in future editions of this book.

ADVENTURE IS Out there

WELBECK

Written by Jenni Lazell

Illustrated by Tjarda Borsboom

Contents

Seeking adventure?

If you're looking for a little adventure in your life, you've come to the right place!

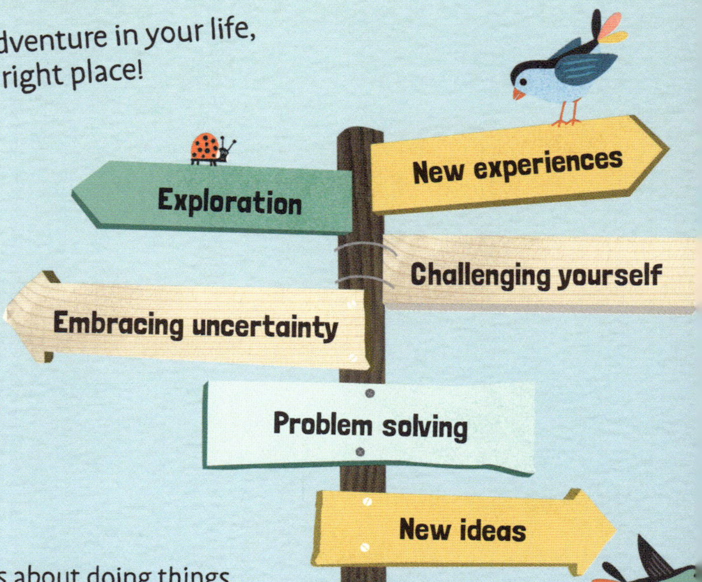

What is adventure?

When you think of adventure, you might imagine someone trekking in some remote part of the world, but adventure is not all about thrill-seeking. It doesn't have to be extreme. Adventure can be in the small things, like the first time you rode a bike, or cooked a meal from scratch.

Adventure is about doing things you wouldn't normally do, facing new experiences head-on, and the willingness to see the world from a different perspective. Adventure is all around us, at all times, we need only to seek it out.

What's inside?

Within these pages, you'll find creative challenges, practical advice, support for learning new skills, space to document your thoughts and findings, and so much more. Dive into the pages that call you, or work through them one by one. Are you ready? Adventure is out there!

"To live would be an awfully big adventure."
– Peter Pan

WHAT DOES ADVENTURE MEAN TO YOU?

"The voyage of discovery is not in seeking new landscapes but in having new eyes."
–Thomas Alva Edison

"Adventure is worthwhile in itself."
– Amelia Earhart

Animal identification guide

Use this handy guide when out and about to investigate which animals have left their mark.

Canines

Canines (dogs, wolves and foxes) have oval-shaped paws, with four, large toe prints on each paw and claws marks.

Hooved animals

All hoof prints look very similar but vary in size. Hooves are made of the same stuff as your fingernails, and form two oblong impressions in the ground.

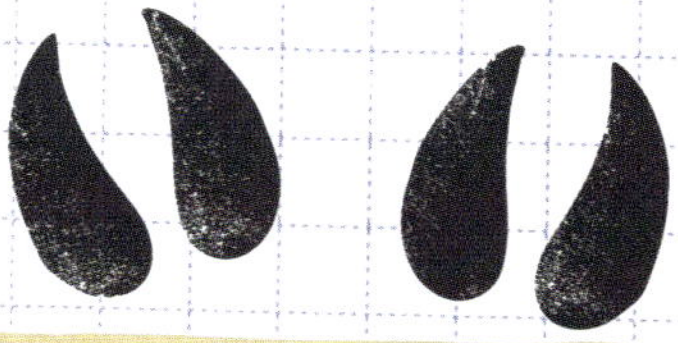

Felines

Felines (house cats, cougars and tigers) have roughly circular paws, with four visible toe prints on each paw and no claw marks. The foot pad looks a bit like the letter M.

Rodents

Rodent (mice, rats, beavers and hamsters) tracks come in all shapes and sizes, but they all show four toes on their front paws and five toes on their back paws.

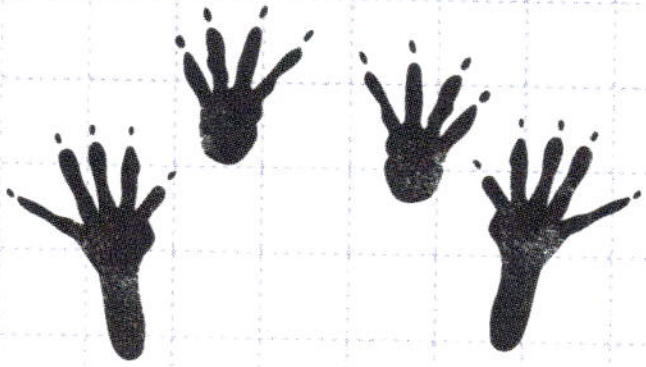

Birds

Most bird tracks show three toes pointing forwards and one long toe pointing backwards. In some birds the back toe is much shorter, or missing altogether.

Reptiles & Amphibians

This group includes a large variety of animals that leave very different tracks. Look out for the snake's long, curved smudge along the ground, or the lizard's distinctive tail drag.

How to build a fire

Learn how to create fire in the wilderness with three of the most common structures.

You will need:

- ★ tinder
- ★ kindling
- ★ fuel wood
- ★ matches

NOTE:
Always ask an adult's permission to make a fire, as well as their help.

Gathering supplies

Tinder: dry fallen leaves, newspaper, grass, or tree bark.

Kindling: dry twigs and small branches about the width of a pencil.

Fuel wood: larger fallen branches or logs.

Clearing a space

First, clear an area on the ground where you want to place your fire. It should be on bare earth to prevent the fire from spreading.

TEEPEE

Also known as a Pyramid fire, this structure looks a bit like a teepee, used by certain Native American tribes.

1. Place your bundle of tinder in the centre of your campfire space. Then, stack pieces of kindling around the tinder in a teepee shape, with an opening on one side to let air in.
2. Keep adding kindling, then add your larger fuel wood in the same teepee structure. Light your kindling with a match, and watch your fire burn!

LOG CABIN

A criss-cross layout, perfect for roasting marshmallows and tin-foil dinners.

1. Lay two parallel pieces of fuel wood roughly 30 cm apart from each other. Place two more pieces of wood on top in the opposite direction. Build the base so it's four layers high.
2. Place your tinder inside the structure and create an inner teepee structure with the kindling.
3. Once you've created the inner teepee, finish the log cabin structure off by placing smaller sticks in a criss-cross manner. Strike a match!

Put out the spark

Fire takes longer to put out than you might think, so start about 20 minutes before you plan to leave. Use a bucket of water to sprinkle on the fire and stir the embers with a stick so all the ashes get wet. Don't leave until the coals are cool to the touch.

SMOKE SIGNALS

Years ago, people used fire to create smoke signals – one of the oldest forms of long distance communication.

Soldiers on the Great Wall of China used smoke signals to warn of attackers.

STAR

You can use this structure if you can't find a lot of wood and want your fire to burn slowly.

1. Place at least three pieces of fuel wood in a star formation, leaving a gap in the middle for the tinder.
2. Add your tinder bundle to the centre of the star, and pile some kindling on top, ensuring enough air can get to the tinder. Light it up!

Campfire cooking

Create these delicious and simple desserts to cook on the campfire.

You will need:

- ★ banana
- ★ chocolate chips or chopped up chocolate bar
- ★ extra toppings of your choice
- ★ tin foil

Banana boat

1

Using a knife, carefully slice down the middle of your banana, keeping the banana in the peel. Then, open it up slightly so it looks a bit like a boat.

2

You could also add other tasty toppings, such as butterscotch or caramel sauce.

Sprinkle chocolate chips (or bits of chocolate bar) into the banana, along with any other tasty toppings of your choice.

3

Wrap your dessert banana tightly in tin foil. Place in the hot charcoal, away from any flames for about ten minutes. You can eat it right out of the foil, but be careful you don't burn your fingers!

That's bananas!

Bananas can help soothe the itch of bug bites and stings. Next time you get bitten, try rubbing a banana peel on the affected area for about 5–10 minutes.

Chocolate fondue s'mores

You will need:

- ★ milk
- ★ chocolate bars broken up into little pieces
- ★ digestive biscuits or vanilla wafers
- ★ marshmallows
- ★ camp cooking pot
- ★ long skewers (or sticks)

1

Pour roughly one third of a cup of milk into a small cooking pot. Place over the hot charcoal away from the flames and bring to a simmer. Heat the milk for about five minutes, stirring with a spoon.

2

Remove the milk from the coals and add the pieces of chocolate bar. Keep stirring until the chocolate has melted into the milk to create a chocolatey sauce.

3

Using a long skewer or stick, toast your marshmallows, choosing a spot in the fire where there are glowing coals but no leaping flames. Hold the marshmallow about 30 cm above this spot.

4

When perfectly roasted, dip the marshmallow in the warm chocolate fondue. Finally, transfer the chocolatey marshmallow to your choice of biscuit base.

TIP

For perfectly toasted marshmallows, keep turning your skewer every few seconds, until the marshmallow is evenly browned and starts to go gooey.

Go Mothing

Discover all the different types of moths fluttering around at night in your area.

You will need:

- a torch
- a light-coloured or white sheet
- washing line
- pegs

Mesmerising moths

For the best results, choose a mild, moonless night with no wind for this mothing activity.

1

Ask an adult to borrow a white or light-coloured bed sheet. Use some pegs to hang it on the washing line outdoors. You can also drape the sheet over two chairs set apart from each other.

NOTE:
Avoid touching moth wings, as you can damage them easily.

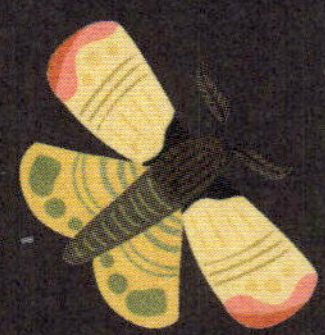

2

Shine a bright torch on as much of the sheet as possible. Moths should start appearing very quickly.

3

Different types of moths will show up at different times in the evening, so keep an eye out for newcomers. Note them down so you can identify them later.

MOTHS AND BUTTERFLIES

The best way to tell the difference between a moth and a butterfly is to look at their antennae.

Moths aren't all just dull brown – these incredible beauties can rival the brightest butterflies!

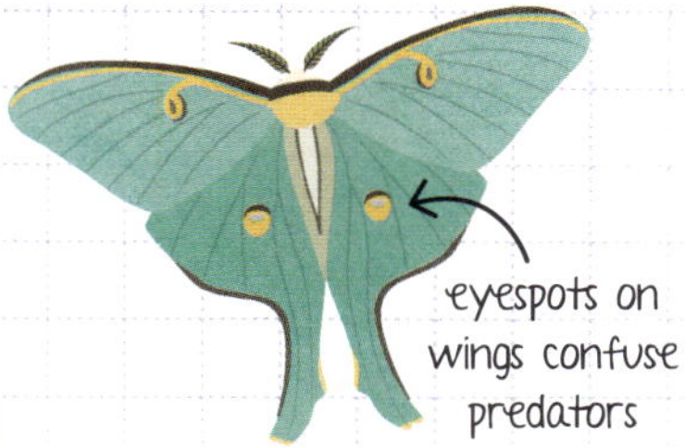

LUNA MOTH
Found in: North America

ELEPHANT HAWK MOTH
Found in: Europe, Asia

ATLAS MOTH
Found in: Asia, Southeast Asia

Make an insect hotel

Create a safe and cosy home for all kinds of bugs.

You will need:

- ★ an old drawer, flowerpot, birdhouse or wooden box
- ★ toilet roll tubes
- ★ a selection of pinecones, twigs, pebbles, moss, bamboo with holes, bark, leaves

Safe shelter

A bug hotel can be used in all seasons to provide a safe space for wandering wildlife. They come in all shapes and sizes, so you don't need to buy anything. You can make it your own.

1

Choose a container for your hotel. This could be a flowerpot, an old birdhouse with the front removed, or even an old wooden drawer. It just needs to be able to withstand bad weather.

2

Gather the supplies to make your hotel with different 'rooms' for your guests. Try finding pebbles, tree bark, twigs, pinecones, moss, straw, toilet roll tubes, and hollow bamboo canes.

BEE OUR GUEST

Consider what type of visitors you want to attract. Use pinecones for ladybirds, bamboo canes for solitary bees, and loose wood for beetles and other bugs.

3. Now use the supplies to pack your chosen container. Keep in mind which insects you want to attract. When the container is full, choose a place to put your hotel, such as a garden or balcony, and wait to see who visits!

Save the bees!

During spring and summer it's not unusual to find bumblebees on the ground. Most of the time they're just resting. If you find a bumblebee on the pavement, use a leaf or twig to move it to safer location.

If a bee remains on the ground for longer than 45 minutes, it might be too tired to move. You can make a special bee energy drink by mixing a half and half solution of water and white sugar.

Put a few drops on a teaspoon or bottle cap next to the bee. This should give it enough of a boost that it can recover and fly away.

How to tie knots

Learn how to master four of the most common knots used in camping, climbing, sailing and other activities.

Clove hitch

This easy knot is used to type a rope to an object, such as a post, pole or a ring.

1. Hang the rope from the support, and loop the end of the rope around it.

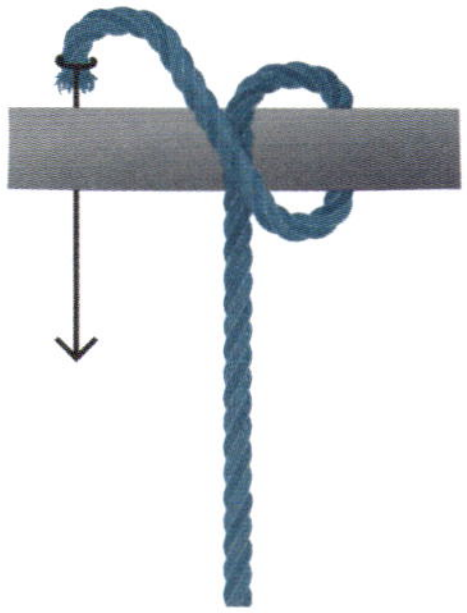

2. Pass the end of the rope up and behind the top rope.

3. Pull each end of the rope to tighten and complete your knot.

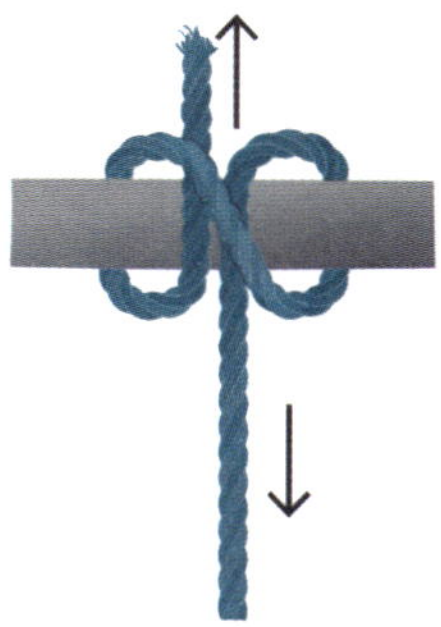

Reef

Also known as the square knot, or Hercules knot. This is a simple way of tying two ropes together.

1. Cross the end of the right length of rope over the left length, as shown.

2. Now cross the end of the left length of rope over the right length.

3. Pull the ends of the ropes to tighten the knot.

KNOT MNEMONIC

Right over left, left over right,
makes a knot both tidy and tight.

Figure 8

A stopper knot, most often used in climbing. Follow the 8 shape again with the end of the rope to create a super secure double figure 8.

1

Bring the end of a length of rope upwards to create a loop.

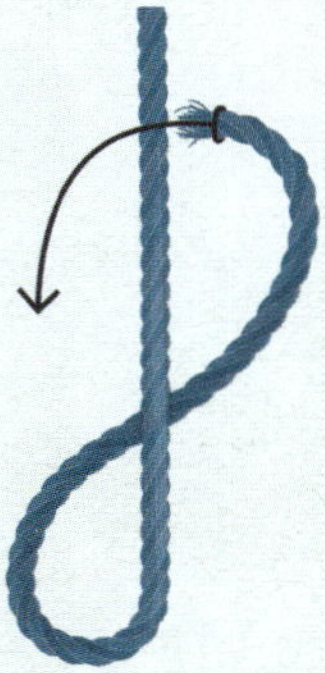

2

Wrap the end of the rope around the back of the main length, and poke the end through the loop.

3

Pull the end of the rope through the loop and pull each end tight to create a knot that looks like the number 8.

KNOT MNEMONIC

First make a hole; the rabbit runs around the tree, and down the hole.

Slip

A quick 'stopper' knot that stops the end of the rope from unravelling. The rope comes free easily when you pull the end.

1

Form a loop near the end of a length of rope.

2

Bring the end of the rope up and wrap it around the loop.

3

Wrap it around again.

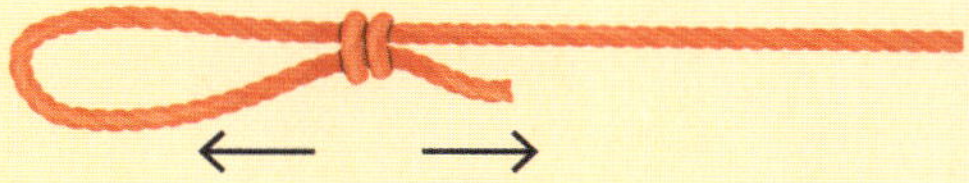

4

Hold the loop and pull the end to tighten the knot.

Be an animal poo detective

Explore another way to track animals by matching each creature to their number two.

The clue is in the poo

Droppings, dung, faeces, excrement, scat, spoor... These are all words to describe animal poo. Which of these have you spotted on your travels?

1

Size: small
Shape: round
Other features: shiny, dark, appears in clusters

2

Size: large
Shape: ranges from oblong to blob
Other features: black, brown, contains seeds and hair

3

Size: small
Shape: oblong
Other features: dark green, smells of eucalyptus

4

Size: small
Shape: splatter
Other features: greenish-white, part solid, part liquid

5

Size: large
Shape: round splat
Other features: soft, brown

Pretend poo

Owls (and other birds) can't digest the bones and fur of their prey, so they have to cough up these parts. Called pellets, they look like droppings, but don't smell.

6

Size: huge
Shape: oblong
Other features: brownish beige, clay-like

A

KOALA

Koalas poo all day, even when they're asleep!

Faecal facts

- Sloths only poo once a week.
- Elephant dung contains so much plant fibre that we can use it to make paper.
- Wombats produce cube-shaped poo.
- Dried bat poo (called guano) was used to make gunpowder.
- Parrotfish poo sand.

B

DEER

When startled, deer will poo before running off.

C

ALLIGATOR

Alligator poo turns white and chalky as it dries.

D

BEAR

In late summer and autumn, you can spot berries in bear poo.

E

MACAW

Bird poo is a mix of wee and poo. The acid in the wee turns some of the mixture white.

F

WATER BUFFALO

Dried water buffalo dung can be burned for fuel.

Answers: 1B, 2D, 3A, 4E, 5F, 6C

Make rock art

Use nature to make some incredible patterns with the materials around you.

No tools needed

Have you ever come across an amazing pattern of stones and wondered who made it? Try it out for yourself! Collect stones that are all different shapes, sizes and colours, or find ones that all look the same. Try including other elements too, such as leaves, pinecones, seeds, or shells.

Balancing act

You can use flat stones to stack on top of each other – river stones are good for this. How high can you stack your stones before they topple over?

MOSAICS

In Ancient Greece and Rome people created incredible pictures on walls or floors made out of tiny pieces of coloured rocks, stones, glass and shells. You can still see these mosaics today!

Rock painting

Have a go at painting on rocks to make some incredible patterns, or 3D art. Use them to decorate your windowsill, or leave them somewhere to surprise others.

Create a treasure map

Guide your friends to hidden treasure.

You will need:

- ★ plain paper
- ★ large tray or bowl
- ★ tea bag or coffee granules
- ★ pens or pencils
- ★ your choice of treasure

Pirate booty

Choose a place to hide some treasure, such as sweets, and craft a map to lead a trail for your friends to follow. Can they find the pirate booty?

1

Take a plain sheet of paper and crumple it to give it an ancient, weathered look. Open it out to flatten it and lay it in the tray.

2

Ask an adult to help you mix the tea or coffee with hot water. Wait for the mixture to cool, then pour it into the tray, over the paper and wait for around ten minutes.

3

Once the the paper has changed colour remove it from the tray and hang it somewhere safe to dry.

4

Tear the edges to make the map look more authentic, or you could ask an adult to burn them.

Once dry, use a pencil to draw your map before going over it in pen.

Here be dragons

On ancient maps there were undiscovered sections. Mapmakers, called cartographers, would fill these sections with strange sea monsters, and other imaginary or mythical creatures.

Give different areas of your map names, like 'Crystal Caves', or 'Whispering Island'.

Draw a compass rose on your map to mark the directions

Build a den

Create a cozy outdoor space where you can hang out with your friends.

Choose a sturdy tree to form the support for your den. Try and find one with a fork low down to rest your branches on.

Rainy days

If you want to use your den in wet weather, you will need to cover it with a waterproof material, such as a tarpaulin.

You can always give your den a coating of mud and leaves to try and keep it water-tight.

Gather long, straight fallen branches to lean against the tree trunk. You can use rope or string to keep the branches from falling down.

Creating castles

Think about how you want to use your den. Is it a meeting place for secret agents, a dwelling for elves, or the perfect place to chill out with a book?

MAKE IT YOUR OWN

Add the finishing touches to your den with decorations, such as pebbles, logs, bricks, outdoor cushions, rugs, blankets, and more.

Navigate using the stars

Learn how constellations can help you find your way, wherever you are.

Star compass

GPS on phones can make it easy to get around, but there's a way to navigate without technology that sailors have used for thousands of years. Use constellations in the night sky to find north, south, east and west in both the northern and southern hemispheres.

NOTE

Stars may seem to move as the Earth rotates, but constellations always appear in the same positions in relation to each other.

Southern hemisphere

SOUTHERN CROSS

Another way to find south is to look for the Crux (or Southern Cross) constellation, a group of five stars. It's the smallest constellation but one of the most important for navigation.

Draw a line with your hand from Gacrux to Acrux and extend it downwards. The end of the line points south. Keep going down until your hand reaches the horizon. East will be on your left, west to your right, and north directly behind you.

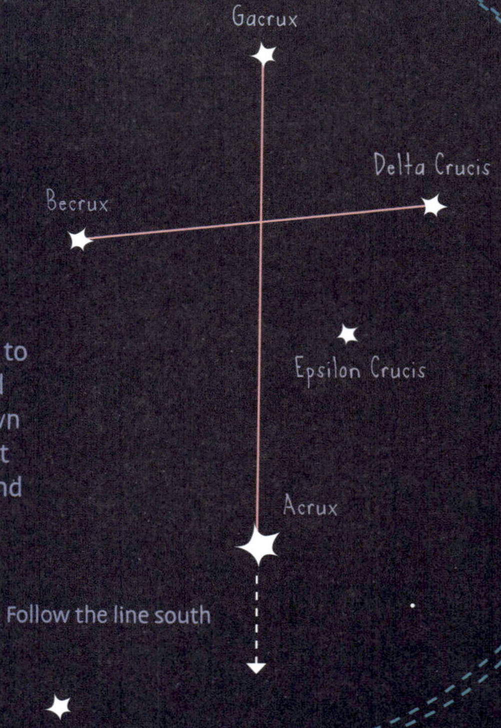

Northern hemisphere

FIND NORTH

Polaris, the North star, sits directly over the North Pole and is the only star to remain fixed in the night sky. You can find it by locating The Plough (or Big Dipper) constellation, and following the two stars at the end of the 'pan' upwards.

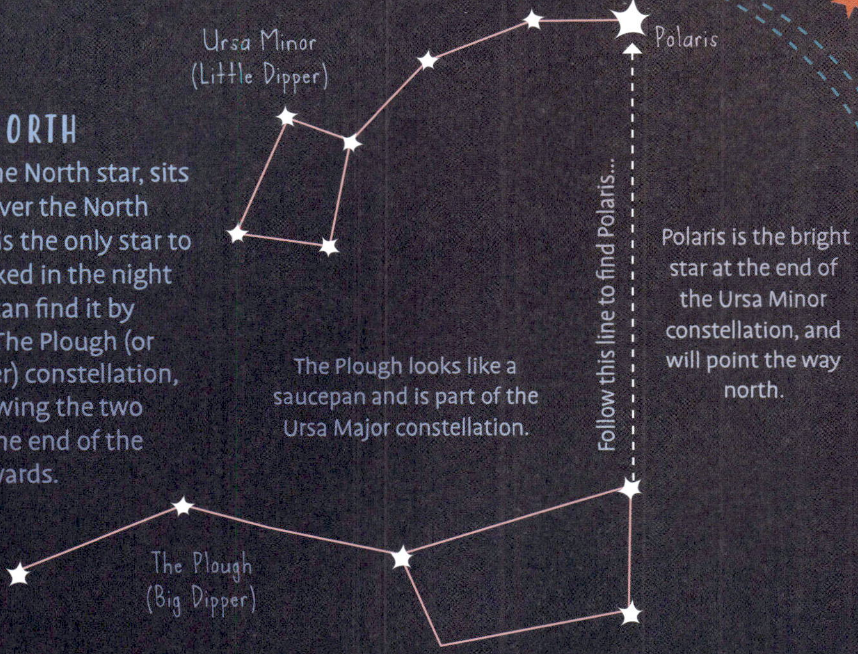

FIND SOUTH

The constellation of Orion, the hunter, can be found by looking for the three stars in a line close together, which form his belt. Orion's sword, or dangling belt strap, points south.

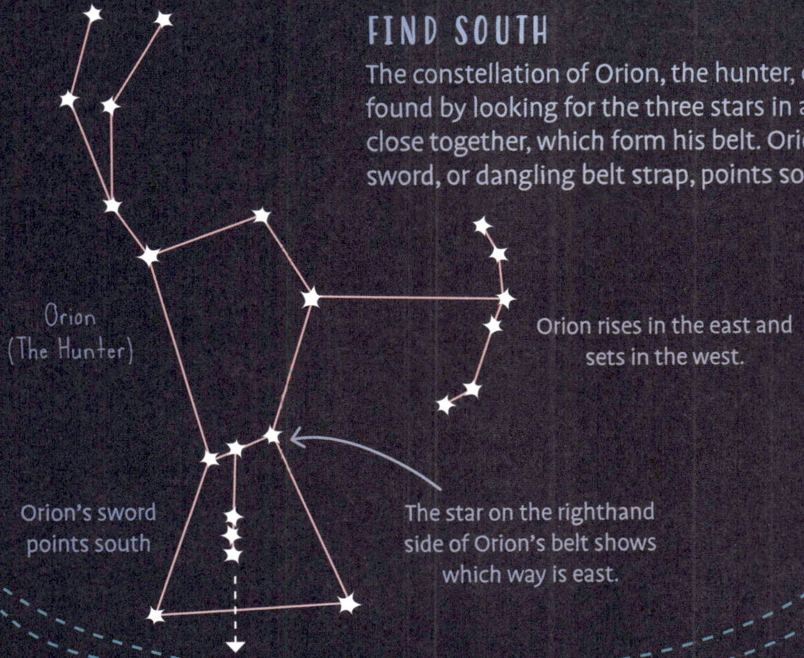

Make a butterfly feeding station

Provide a colourful place for butterflies to find a tasty treat.

You will need:

- ★ plate with a sloping rim
- ★ flower pot hangers or twine
- ★ marbles or small pebbles
- ★ your choice of colourful decorations

Beautiful butterflies

Butterflies help pollinate flowers and vegetable gardens – and with their bright, flashing wings, they're fun to watch, too!

1

Choose an old plate that can hold liquid without spilling, and add some small pebbles or marbles. These are for the butterflies to land on.

2

Attach your flower pot hangers to the plate. You could also look up online how to make a basic macrame cradle for the plate using cord or twine.

3

Butterflies are attracted to colourful things, so decorate your plate and hangers with ribbons, paint, artificial flowers, and more. The brighter the better!

Look out for butterflies at all stages of their lifecycle

Caterpillar
They come in all shapes and sizes. Find these hungry beasties munching their way through leaves.

Pupa
Difficult to spot, caterpillars choose a safe, sheltered place underneath a leaf or twig to form a hardened shell, called a chrysalis.

Adult
After several weeks of transformation, an adult butterfly emerges and dries its wings before taking flight.

Egg
Spot these stuck on leaves and stems.

Butterflies also like overripe and rotting fruit.

You could fill the plate with water instead to create a drinking station for bees, birds and other flying creatures.

4

Hang the plate in a shady spot from a tree branch, or on a balcony. Now fill the plate with nectar and wait to see how many types of butterfly come to visit.

HOW TO MAKE 'NECTAR'

* Mix 1 cup of granulated sugar with 4 cups of water in a large pot.
* Ask an adult for help in heating the solution on the hob and bringing it to the boil.
* Boil until the sugar dissolves and let the solution cool to room temperature before using.

Go foraging

Discover the kinds of food you can find in nature.

Nature's bounty

Foraging means finding and gathering food in the wild for free. Many of the items you find in the supermarket, can also be found growing wild. Here are some of the edible fruit and plants you might find when foraging.

Crab apples

Usually too tart to eat raw, but great cooked in apple crumbles.

Wild garlic

Use leaves in cooking to create a milder garlic flavour.

Dandelions

Use leaves and flowers in salads.

Wild strawberries

Can be eaten right off the stem, or used in many desserts.

Cockles

Edible molluscs found in sandy beaches, boiled and often served with vinegar as a snack.

Mint

Use the leaves in teas, or chew them for a refreshing taste.

Daisies

Good in sandwiches, soups and salads.

Samphire

Salty, seaweed-like plant, found near the coast, that is good with fish.

Not so fungi

Mushrooms (fungi) are great to eat, but some can be deadly. It's difficult to identify which mushrooms are safe, so you should NEVER eat wild mushooms, unless they've been identified by an expert.

FORAGING GUIDELINES

Follow these guidelines when out and about to be a responsible forager.

- Ask an expert to help you identify plants – you need to be absolutely certain you know what they are.
- Some plants should only be eaten at certain times of the year. Bring a guidebook (and an expert) for research.
- Find out where you have permission to forage – public places are usually okay, but it's best to check first.
- Pick a small amount from lots of different places so that the plant will regrow and you leave enough for wildlife.
- Don't forage too close to roads or sources of pollution.

Make nettle tea

Brew a calming mug of tea from stinging nettles.

Springtime is the perfect time to harvest nettle leaves. Use scissors to snip the top few leaves on each young nettle plant, until you have a good pile.

Stinging secrets

The idea of using stinging nettles in food and drinks can be a bit alarming, as this is one plant we usually try to avoid! But stinging nettles are packed with vitamins and minerals, and are surprisingly tasty, too!

TIP

Wear long-sleeved clothes and gardening or rubber gloves when handling nettles so you don't get stung!

1. Once you've harvested your leaves, keep your gloves on and wash the leaves thoroughly in warm water to get rid of any bugs, dirt and other plants.

2. Ask an adult to help you fill a pot with three cups of water and place on the hob to boil. Add one cup of fresh leaves and simmer for about five minutes. Boiling the leaves removes the sting.

3. Strain your tea into a mug using a seive. Add a spoonful of honey to taste, and enjoy your nettle tea.

Stinging nettles are covered in tiny, hollow hairs that act like needles when touched, and push chemicals through to your skin.

Go blackberrying

Explore woodland and hedgerows to find these juicy berries bursting with flavour.

Picking time

The best time to go blackberrying is late summer to early autumn. The berries start off red, but when ripe they will deepen to a dark purpley-black colour. A ripe blackberry will come off the stem easily, if you have to tug at it then it's not ready.

If any blackberries make it home, you can serve them with yoghurt for breakfast, or make a range of delicious desserts, such as blackberry crumble. Just make sure to wash them before you eat them.

Mind the thorns!

Make sure you bring lots of pails or baskets for your berrypicking.

TIP

Avoid picking berries that are too close to the ground, as this is perfect peeing height for dogs!

Which animal adventurer are you?

Take this quiz to find out which animal best represents your adventurous soul.

1 On the weekend, you can find me...

A. At home, snuggled on the sofa.
B. Trying out a new recipe.
C. Hosting a great party with my friends.
D. Checking my diary, I have places to be.

2 Someone dared me to go skydiving...

A. Nope. No way, I'm not crazy.
B. Maybe, if I get paid.
C. I'll do it, but only if my friends do too.
D. Let's go! What are you waiting for?

3 My favourite season is...

A. Winter.
B. Autumn.
C. Summer.
D. Spring.

4 If I could travel anywhere, I would go...

A. A good book can take you all over the world.
B. Somewhere I can speak the language.
C. Somewhere new and exciting.
D. To outer space.

5 My favourite flavour of ice-cream is...

A. Vanilla.
B. Salted caramel.
C. Rocky road.
D. Maple syrup & bacon.

6 My wardrobe essential is...

A. A onesie.
B. Sunglasses.
C. Sequins.
D. Hiking boots.

7 I'm going to paint my bedroom...

A. Cool blue
B. Leafy green
C. Sunset red
D. Bright yellow

Mostly As

You're a

BEAVER

Your home is your castle! Why go anywhere else? You can make your home as exciting as can be with the company of your family, and a little DIY. You don't need to travel across the world to have an adventure, but make sure to stay open to new experiences.

Mostly Bs

You're a

CAT

Just like a curious feline, you like to check out new places. But then again, you also enjoy a long snooze in the sunshine at home. Planning fun activities can be a little tiring, but don't give up on your ideas.

Mostly Cs

You're a

DOLPHIN

Dolphins roam the seas in groups of family and friends, called pods. Super playful, you have tons of energy for exploration and love to try new things. But don't be afraid to discover cool places and activities on your own.

Mostly Ds

You're an

ALBATROSS

You go wherever the wind takes you! Like the albatross, you like to always be on the move, free like a bird, and barely ever touch down in one place. Make sure you take some time to rest and relax, too.

Step forward, brave adventurer

Imagine a journalist wants to interview you, what would you say?

Draw or cut and stick a profile picture of you here.

What three words describe you best?

....

....

....

Who would you take with you on all your adventures? Why would they make the best adventuring partner?

....

....

....

....

....

....

....

What's your favourite quote?

....

....

....

What's your favourite season, and why?

....

....

....

Do you prefer…

Circle your answer.

sweet or salty?

cozy fire or hot sunshine?

plans or spontaneity?

ketchup or mayonnaise?

night or day?

running or hiking?

pancakes or waffles?

stay in or go out?

book or movie?

singing or dancing?

rain or snow?

starter or dessert?

What makes you excited?

....

....

....

....

....

....

....

....

....

....

What have been your best adventures so far?

....

....

....

....

....

....

....

....

Tell a spooky campfire story

Learn how to thrill everyone around the fire with your spine-tingling stories.

Campfire performance

A true campfire story isn't just about what you say, but how you say it. To really spook your friends, you will need to use your posture, expressions and your voice to bring the story to life.

TIP

Shine a torch up at your face to create creepy shadows as you stare into your audience's eyes.

SETTING THE SCENE

Did you just hear a noise in the woods? Was it an animal... or something much worse? Before starting your story, build suspense by drawing everyone's attention to the spooky darkness beyond the campfire.

•

The tale you're about to tell is a true story. Hand on heart. 'True' stories make people think that the same things that happened in the tale could also happen to them. Eek!

Storyteller advice

Be serious – nothing ruins a good scary story like laughing in the middle of it! Practice keeping a straight face.

MAKING A MONSTER

There is a monster at the heart of every scary story. This could be an actual monster, a ghost, an alien, or even something that ***seems*** quite ordinary and innocent.

Keep the details vague. It's always scarier when at first you only get little hints and glimpses. This helps to create uncertainty and fear that increases as the story goes on.

The story might end when you reveal your monster in all its terrifying glory. Maybe your characters fight it off, or the monster escapes. Perhaps it's still out there... waiting.

ACT IT OUT

Varying the volume and speed of your voice can dramatically change the feel of your tale. Speed up during moments of intense action and slow down, using a soft voice, sound effects and dramatic pauses, "knock... knock... knock..." to create enough tension for the best jump scare: "BOO!"

Senses

We experience the world through our senses. For the most vivid story, don't forget to describe each one.

Sight

Sound

Touch

Taste

Smell

rats storms strange noises

venomous spiders powercuts howling wind echoing footsteps tombstones

Create a campfire story

Use this space to come up with your own chilling tale.

TIP

Make sure your story has a clear beginning, middle and end.

abandoned houses vampires creaky doors screams

bats portraits with moving eyes werewolves ghouls

sharks

talking dolls

snapping twigs

cobwebs

moving shadows

Other words for scary

PETRIFYING
SPOOKY
TERRIFYING
CREEPY
EERIE
NERVE-WRACKING
SINISTER
HAUNTING
BLOOD-CURDLING

snakes moonlight

Go birdwatching

See how many different types of birds you can spot.

Eagle eyes

Birds are everywhere – they're the easiest form of wildlife to get to know. Get out your binoculars and draw or take pictures of how many different types of bird you see around you.

Fastest animal on Earth!

Peregrine falcon

Found in: countries worldwide

Eurasian Magpie

Found in: Europe, Asia

Cardinal

Found in: North & South America

Super soft feathers for silent flying

Barn owl

Found in: countries worldwide

Kingfisher

Found in: Europe, Asia, North Africa

Sulphur crested cocktaoo

Found in: Australia, Southeast Asia

Atlantic puffin

Found in: Europe, North America

Grey heron

Found in: Europe, Asia, Africa

Smallest type of bird

Hummingbird

Found in: the Americas

Mimicry

Australia's Superb Lyrebird can imitate any sound, from other bird calls to chainsaws, camera shutters, fire alarms, and dog barks. Check it out online!

Feed the birds

Provide a winter treat for birds with a homemade feeder.

You will need:

- ★ a large pinecone
- ★ string or twine
- ★ mixing bowl
- ★ birdseed
- ★ raisins
- ★ lard or suet

1

Choose a large, dried pinecone and tie a length of string or twine around the top. Make sure it's tied tight!

2

In a mixing bowl, use your hands to combine your birdseed and raisins with chopped up pieces of room temperature lard, or suet. Mix until all the birdseed sticks to the fat.

3

Push the mixture into all the small spaces and layer it up to completely cover the cone

Now add the sticky mixture to the pinecone. Once complete, pop your pinecone in the fridge for an hour or so, to harden the fat.

4

Use a clove hitch knot (see page 18) to hang your feeder up outside near a window. Watch which birds come to try it out.

NOTE

Super smart crows are known to bring gifts to the people who feed them regularly. The gifts are usually objects like rocks, bones, keys and dropped earrings.

Cloudspotting

Learn to recognise different cloud types and predict the weather!

Types of cloud

Clouds come in many different shapes and sizes. They're often split into two groups that describe their appearance; cumulus means "heap" and stratus means "sheet".

SHAPESHIFTING CLOUDS

On a warm summer's day you can pick a grassy outdoor space to lay back and gaze up at the sky. Watch the clouds race by – what can you see? A ship, a dragon, or a herd of horses... Invent a story using the shapes you see in the clouds!

Set up a scavenger hunt

See if your friends can find every item on your list.

The hunt is on

A scavenger hunt is a game where people have to try and find everything on a list in a set amount of time. You will need to print enough copies of the list for each person or team, and send everyone off in different directions.

Picture proof

For this hunt, people will need to take a photo of everything on the list. Make sure everyone has a camera or a phone they can use to take pictures.

- ☐ THE BIGGEST STICK
- ☐ A SPIDER WEB
- ☐ SOMETHING BEGINNING WITH R
- ☐ SOMETHING SPARKLY
- ☐ SOMEONE WALKING THEIR DOG
- ☐ THREE DIFFERENT TYPES OF BIRD
- ☐ ANIMAL TRACKS
- ☐ A PINECONE
- ☐ A NEST
- ☐ SOMETHING YELLOW
- ☐ A SEED
- ☐ A STATUE
- ☐ A BENCH
- ☐ THE WEIRDEST SHAPED CLOUD
- ☐ A SNAIL

On other hunts, you might want people to gather the items on the list instead.

Rewards

Think of a good prize for the winners to reward their hard work as they raced around and beat the clock!

DESIGN YOUR OWN

Make a list of some more item ideas here, or write down clues for your friends to puzzle over. Consider your chosen location when you create your list, so you don't have people searching for seashells in a forest!

Rainy day hunts

On a rainy day you could do an indoor scavenger hunt. Try giving your hunt a theme, such as the ocean, or medieval, and base the items on your list around it.

Build an obstacle course

Set up a thrilling course for you and your friends to jump, run and crawl through.

TIP
Use chalk or tape to mark out your course or write instructions.

Obstacle engineer

Get inspired by these obstacle activities and work with whatever materials you can find inside and outside your home.

Activity spots

Set up areas where you have to perform certain activities. This could be something like throwing a ball into a bucket or dancing on the spot. You could also get someone to assign actions to you, 'Simon Says' style.

THE FLOOR IS LAVA

If the rain makes your obstacle course too slippery, you can always try to build one at home. Pretend that the floor is made of lava, and see how far you can travel around the room without touching the ground!

See if you can get through the web without getting in a tangle!

Time it!

Once you've got to grips with your course, it's time to ramp up the challenge level and see who can run it fastest! Use a stopwatch and see if you can break your speed record.

Make a hammock

Craft a cozy, outdoor relaxation space.

You will need:

- ★ bedsheet
- ★ paracord
- ★ long rope
- ★ two sturdy trees

1

Ask your adult to borrow an old bedsheet and fold it in half lengthways.

2

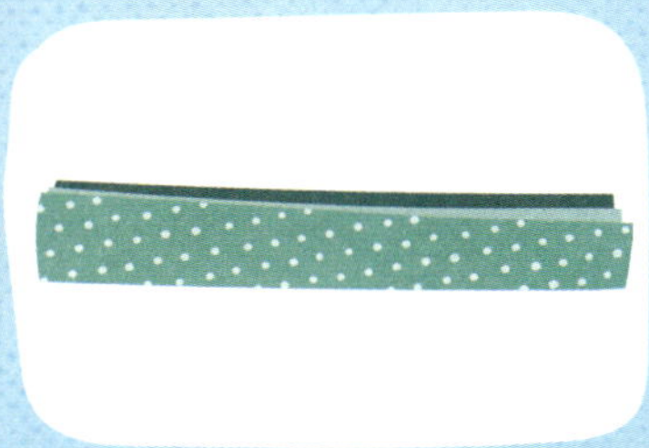

Keep folding the sheet lengthways, until the sheet is 15 cm wide.

3

Fold the end of the sheet down about 30 cm and wrap your paracord around it tightly about 10 times. Use a double knot to secure it.

4

Create a loop in a length of rope and push it through the opening at the end of the sheet.

5

Pass the loose ends of the rope through the looped section of rope and pull the rope tightly. Repeat steps 3 to 5 on the other end of the sheet.

6

Now you need to tie each end of your hammock to two sturdy tree trunks not too far apart from each other.

Check out page 18 for help with knots.

7

Once both ends are secure, you can open up the sheet to reveal your homemade hammock.

Wind in the trees

Birds flitting about

Mindful moments

To appreciate your amazing adventuring, it's important to take the time to relax and be still. Pay attention to the moment. While resting in your hammock, use each of your senses to take note of the world around you.

Soft blanket

Cool drink

Scent of wildflowers and grass

Discover trees

Tree types

There's thousands of varieties, but trees fall into two main groups – deciduous and coniferous. Deciduous trees drop and grow new leaves every year, while coniferous trees hold onto them all year round, which gives them the nickname, evergeen.

Deciduous

Coniferous

Mighty giant

The tallest tree in the world is the Coast redwood. It can reach 115 metres tall, and its trunk can grow to a whopping nine metres in diameter!

Counting rings

When a tree is cut down, you can tell how old it was by counting its rings. One light ring plus one dark ring counts as one year of the tree's life.

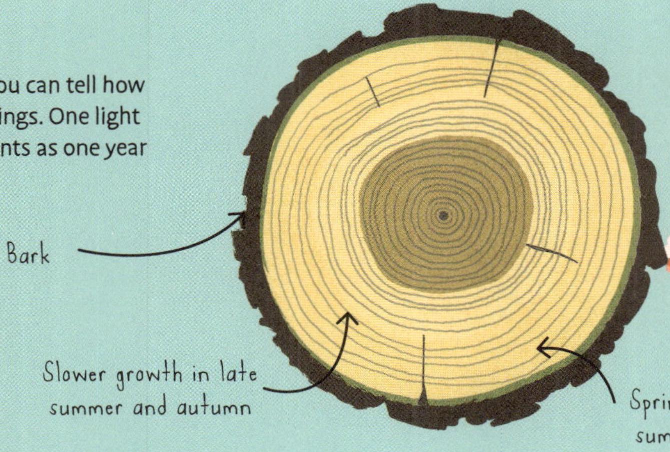

Seeds

See how many different types of tree seeds you can discover. Sometimes they have wings to help transport them through the air, while others are hidden in a spiky case.

PLANT A TREE

Join the battle against climate change by planting trees. Trees absorb carbon dioxide and other air pollution and release oxygen.

Forest bathing

Try the mindful technique of forest bathing. Taking the time to quietly pay attention to the trees and wildlife around you can be a wonderful way to relax.

Create leaf art

Experiment with different ways you can make art from leaves.

You will need:

- ★ leaves
- ★ thick art paper
- ★ white crayons
- ★ paintbrush
- ★ watercolour paints

Leaf rubbing

Try this twist on a traditional leaf rubbing art project using white crayon and watercolours.

1

Gather a selection of leaves. Place a leaf underneath your paper and rub your white crayon over it. It can be hard to tell where you're rubbing, but keep trying.

2

Move the leaf to another place under the paper, or choose another leaf. Keep rubbing the crayon over each new leaf location until you've filled the paper.

3

Now comes the fun bit. Use lots of water and watercolour paints to paint a thin, colourful wash of paint over the paper. The wax crayon will resist the paint and your leaves will suddenly appear.

TIP

Choose leaves with prominent veins. This will make your art stand out on the paper.

Have a go at creating another masterpiece with different types of leaves and coloured backgrounds.

Leaf printing

Use textured leaves with paint to create a stunning print effect.

1

Paint the underside of a large leaf with whatever paints you have to hand, watercolours work well.

2

Carefully press the leaf onto a piece of paper for a few seconds, and slowly peel it away to reveal your leafy print. Try covering the page with lots of different leaves.

Leaf collages

Art doesn't have to be all about paint. Gather leaves together in shapes and patterns to create a collage. Combine leaves with sketches to create some fun, leafy animals.

Adventure bucket list

Which of these adventurous activities would you like to try?

- [ ] Coasteering
- [ ] Watch the sun rise

- [ ] Mountain biking

Tick all that apply:

- [ ] Scuba diving
- [ ] Hike up a mountain
- [ ] Paragliding
- [ ] Go to a festival
- [ ] Watch the sun rise
- [ ] Horse riding
- [ ] Try a new food

- [ ] Plant some trees
- [ ] Sleep under the stars
- [ ] Cook food on a campfire
- [ ] Be a tourist in your home town
- [ ] Start a new hobby

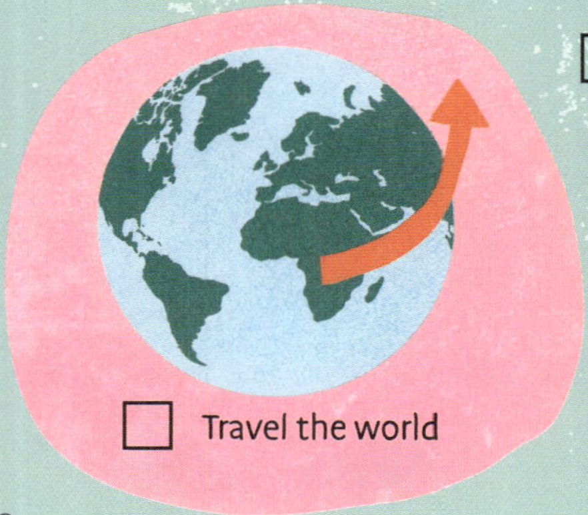

- [ ] Travel the world
- [ ] Go on safari
- [ ] Climbing
- [ ] Sailing
- [ ] Skiing
- [ ] See the polar lights

- [ ] Lake fishing

- [ ] Perform a random act of kindness
- [ ] Fossil hunting
- [ ] Skydiving
- [ ] Caving
- [ ] Bungee jumping
- [ ] Roll down a hill

- [ ] Go on a bat walk
- [ ] Surfing

- [ ] Visit a desert island
- [ ] Go on a road trip
- [ ] Visit a national park
- [ ] Ride a scary rollercoaster
- [ ] Kayaking
- [ ] Take part in a carnival
- [ ] Swim with sharks

- [ ] Grow your own veg
- [ ] Trek through the jungle
- [ ] Learn a new language

MAKE A LIST OF ANY OTHER ACTIVITES YOU'D LIKE TO TRY

Survive a desert island

Take this quiz to discover if you have what it takes to stay alive.

1 So, here you are, alone on a desert island. What now?

A. This is a nightmare! Where's my phone?
B. Time to explore this island.
C. Start gathering any useful items from the wreck.

2 You're so parched!

A. Good thing there's plenty of water in the sea, right?
B. I found these coconuts – that's food AND water.
C. I'm collecting rainwater and have found a nearby river.

3 It's getting dark...

A. It's scary. At least I have Derek. The coconut.
B. I have great night vision.
C. I better try and build a fire.

HERE'S THE PRIORITY ORDER IF YOU DO GET STRANDED ON A DESERT ISLAND:

1. Find a water source
2. Build shelter
3. Make a fire
4. Find food
5. Signal for help
6. Create tools

Mostly As

HMM

Welp. You made your choices. Unfortunately, they weren't very good ones. You might be stuck here a while. Or not...

4 Where are you going to sleep?

A. Who can sleep at a time like this?
B. Under the stars, I can try a different spot every night.
C. I've built a lean-to shelter against this tree.

5 Was that your stomach growling?

A. I ate these berries I found, but now I feel a bit iffy.
B. I'm trying a coconut-based diet right now.
C. I'm waiting for this fish I caught to cook on the fire.

6 It must be pretty lonely by now.

A. Derek is a hoot! But I can tell he's feeling a bit stressed.
B. Nah, I'm making friends with the local wildlife.
C. I'll just keep focusing on the next step.

7 How about a rescue signal?

A. I've been yelling for hours! HELP!!
B. Who needs rescuing? I've got it all under control.
C. I've spelled out 'SOS' on the beach with sticks and stones.

Mostly Bs

SURVIVING

What another beautiful day. It's so peaceful here, you've got everything you need. Well, you're still alive, but you're no expert. It might be time to seek help.

Mostly Cs

GOING HOME

The plane saw your message, thank goodness – you're saved! It's a good thing you stayed calm and concentrated on the important things.

Phases of the moon

Track the moon's changing shape in each month.

Waxing or waning

You can tell if the moon is waxing or waning based on its shape. For those that live in the Northern hemisphere, the shape of a waxing (growing) moon resembles the letter D, and a waning moon the letter C. But this is reversed if you live in the Southern hemisphere.

Shapes and shadows

We can only ever see one side of the moon, so people have become familiar with all its markings. In the dark patches of the moon people have seen faces, trees, men and women, hands, animals and more... What can you spot in the moon's rocky surface?

Supermoons

A supermoon takes place when the moon is closest to the Earth. It can appear as much as 30 per cent brighter and up to 15 per cent larger than a regular full moon.

MOON TYPES

There are 12 named full moons in a year. A blue moon refers to a second full moon in a calendar month.

JANUARY: Wolf moon
FEBRUARY: Snow moon
MARCH: Worm moon
APRIL: Pink moon
MAY: Flower moon
JUNE: Strawberry moon
JULY: Thunder moon
AUGUST: Sturgeon moon
SEPTEMBER: Corn moon
OCTOBER: Hunter's moon
NOVEMBER: Frost moon
DECEMBER: Cold moon

Moon madness

The full moon has often been linked to strange behaviour; the word 'lunacy' comes from the Latin word for moon, 'luna'. It could explain the myth of werewolves – humans that change into wolves under the light of a full moon.

Great adventurers

Be inspired by these famous explorers and adventurers.

Amelia Earhart

Amelia Earhart flew solo across the Atlantic Ocean in 1932. On a later planned adventure round the world, she and her aircraft disappeared, and have never been found.

To boldly go

The first great adventurers discovered new lands and mapped the world. But that has never stopped people from wanting to explore the world in new and exciting ways, and break some world records in the process.

Sacagawea

In 1803–1806, a Native American girl called Sacagawea guided explorers Lewis and Clark as they mapped out areas of North America.

Thor Heyerdahl

Thor Heyerdahl successfully sailed across the Pacific Ocean from South America to the Polynesian Islands on a wooden raft, in 1947, just to prove that it could be done.

Sir Ranulph Fiennes

Ranulph Fiennes is considered to be the 'greatest living explorer'. He was the first to reach both Poles, discovered a lost city, and ran seven marathons in seven days on seven continents.

Steve Fossett

In 2002, Steve Fossett broke the record for flying around the world nonstop in any aircraft. He chose a balloon that used both hot air and gas to make the journey, which took 13 days.

Junko Tabei

While Edmund Hillary and Tenzing Norgay were the first to climb Everest, the incredible Junko Tabei was the first woman to make the ascent, and she went on to climb the highest peak on every continent.

Nellie Bly

In 1889, journalist Nellie Bly beat the record of the fictional novel *Around the World in 80 Days* by travelling round the world by train and ship in only 72 days.

Jacques Piccard

In 1960, Jacques Piccard explored the dark depths of the North Pacific ocean in his deepsea submersible, *Trieste*. He descended 10,911 m into the Mariana trench, and discovered new life on the seabed.

Make a sundial

Tell the time using the position of the sun.

You will need:

- ★ a sunny day
- ★ a long stick
- ★ 12 stones or pebbles
- ★ a watch

Ancient clocks

Before we had clocks and electronics, people used sundials to tell the time. Sundials measure time by the position of the sun and the direction of shadows.

TIP

Start this activitiy early in the morning!

1

Wedge a long stick into the ground so it stands upright.

The bit that casts a shadow on a sundial is called a gnomon.

2

Look at your watch, and when it reaches the hour, use a stone to mark the position of the stick's shadow.

3

Keep observing over the course of the day. At each hour, mark the exact spot the shadow falls with a stone.

Did you know?

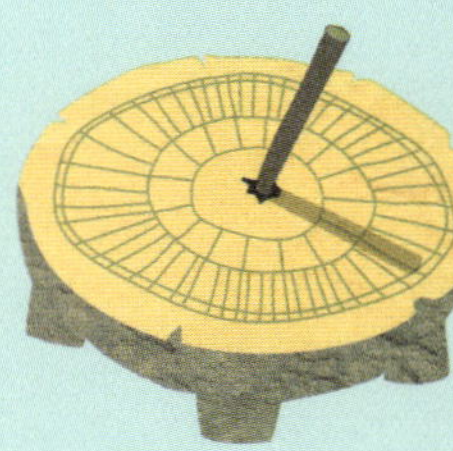

The earliest known sundial was made by Ancient Egyptians.

Make a weather vane

See which way the wind blows.

You will need:

- a windy day
- card
- pen
- drinking straw
- scissors
- pencil with a rubber top
- pin
- modelling clay (or adhesive putty)

1

On a square piece of card, mark each of the compass directions. Stick a blob of modelling clay to the centre of the card, and push a pencil into the modelling clay.

2

Use scissors to cut a notch at either end of a drinking straw. On another piece of card, cut out a triangle and a rectangle piece of card. This is the head and tail of your arrow. Slot them into each end of the straw.

3

Push a pin through the centre of the straw and into the rubber end of your pencil. Which way is the wind blowing?

Make note of the wind's direction for a week. Does it blow one way more than another?

How to remember the directions of the compass:

N Naughty
E Elephants
S Squirt
W Water

Give geology a go

Learn about different rocks and minerals and how they are formed.

The Moon is ma
of igneous rock

Collecting rocks

A geologist studies the structure of the Earth, including rocks, minerals, mountains and volcanoes. There are three different categories of rock: igneous, sedimentary and metamorphic. How many different types of rocks can you collect?

Basalt sometimes forms in tall hexagonal columns.

Igneous

Igneous comes from the Latin word for fire. These rocks form when molten rock, known as magma or lava, cools and hardens.

Examples: granite, obsidian, basalt
Where to find: volcanic and mountain regions or deep underground

Sedimentary

Sedimentary rocks are made from fragments of other rocks, minerals and sand that are carried to one place by wind or water and squished together in layers over many years to form new rocks.

Examples: limestone, sandstone, shale
Where to find: coasts and near bodies of water

The Great Sphinx in Egypt was carved from limestone over 4,500 years ago.

You can find fossils trapped in sedimentary rocks.

Metamorphic

Metamorphic rocks start out as either igneous or sedimentary rocks that are slowly changed into a new type of rock due to heat and pressure. They often have a stripy appearance.

Examples: marble, gneiss, slate
Where to find: mountain ranges and deep underground

Birth Stones

Some cultures think there is a lucky gemstone for each month..

EARTH'S ROCKY SECRETS

A lot of gemstones just look like coloured rock until they are cut, shaped and polished until they sparkle and shine. The word crystal comes from the Greek word *kyros*, which means 'icy cold'.

JANUARY:
Garnet

FEBRUARY:
Amethyst

MARCH:
Aquamarine

APRIL:
Diamond or Quartz

MAY:
Emerald

JUNE:
Moonstone

JULY:
Ruby

AUGUST:
Peridot

SEPTEMBER:
Sapphire

OCTOBER:
Tourmaline or Opal

NOVEMBER:
Citrine or Topaz

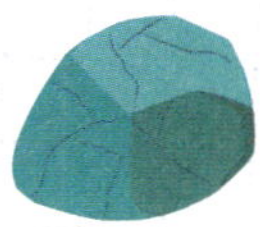

DECEMBER:
Turquoise

Dig for fossils

Hunt for fossils along the coast.

What are fossils?

Fossils are the preserved remains, imprints or traces of living things from millions of years ago, such as bones, teeth, shells, eggs and footprints. Fossils have been found on every continent on Earth, most often along the coast, where the water erodes the rock. See what you can spot!

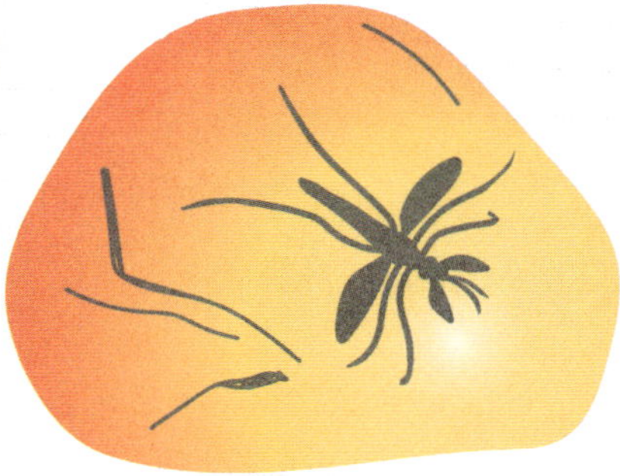

Amber

Some ancient plants and insects have been perfectly preserved in resin – a sticky tree sap that hardens into amber.

Digging up the past

The study of dinosaur fossils is called palaeontology. It can take hours of hard work with trowels and brushes to reveal the brittle bones of dinosaurs. Most of the time the skeleton isn't perfectly laid out, so palaeontologists have to reassemble bones like a jigsaw.

Make your own fossils

Create your own fossils using salt dough.

You will need:

- ★ 1 cup salt
- ★ 1 cup flour
- ★ mixing bowl
- ★ parchment paper
- ★ something to make an imprint

Making a mark

You can make your own fossil to show how prehistoric creatures might have sunk into mud that turned into rock. When their body dissolved, it left an impression in the ground.

1

Add half of the salt to your flour and mix them together. Then slowly add water and start mixing. Keep adding water and salt until the dough is firm and not too sticky.

2

Take some of the dough and roll it into a ball, then place it onto a piece of parchment paper and squish the ball to create a flattened pancake of dough.

3

Now choose an object to make an imprint with. This could be a shell, a leaf, a toy dinosaur, or something else. Press it into the dough. When you lift it away it will have left an impression on the dough.

TIP

Paint over the dried dough with cold coffee to give your fossil a more aged and earthy look.

4

Leave your dough to dry for a few days, or bake it in the oven for 20 minutes at 180 °C (350 °F).

Mythical creatures

Look beyond the ordinary to seek signs of supernatural beings.

Fantastic beasts

Mythical monsters or merely misunderstood? Some say these creatures from folklore are alive in the wilderness today, but incredibly skilled at hiding from humans. You'll have to hone your senses to spot one.

Fairies are thought to be repelled by iron.

Fairy

Small, sometimes winged creatures, that are known to be tricksters. Avoid stepping into a circle of mushrooms, this is known as a fairy ring, and is meant to trap you.

Gnome

These small beings live underground and are thought to move through earth as easily as water. They are attacted to shiny things and gems from the earth.

Dryad

Shy, elusive tree spirits, dryads live as long as the tree they are bound to. You might sense their calm presence in forests, or in the whispering of leaves.

In Japan, dryads are known as Kodama, and are shapeshifters.

Troll

Thought to dwell in mountains or caves, trolls are unfriendly towards humans. They avoid the daylight, as it turns them to stone. Look out for large, interesting-shaped rocks that could've been unwary trolls.

Yeti

A huge, ape-like creature with white, shaggy fur, found in the Himalayan mountains. Travellers have often come across its massive footsteps in the snow.

Mermaids lure people through their enchanting song.

Mermaid

There have been many potential sightings of mermaids all over the world. Featuring the head and upper body of a human and the tail of a fish, they are thought to be both friendly and malicious.

A kelpie is also a shape-shifting water horse, but it isn't as deadly as the Each-wisge.

Each-wisge

Next time you see a lone, friendly horse near a body of water, think again: it could be a water horse. If you mount it, you will quickly be galloped to a watery grave.

Wildlife watch

See which animals you can spot out and about.

Animal observer

Use this space to observe what animals you see in nature. Go out in the day, then go out again in the evening – can you spot any different animals? Sketch them here, or stick in your best photos.

Write down if you can hear any particular animal calls. Can you identify all of them?

Have you ever noticed how the eyes of different animals don't all reflect the same colour when you shine a torch on them?

Hides

Many keen animal watchers and photographers use small camouflaged shelters called 'hides', where they can sit quietly and observe animals without disturbing them.

Be a friend to nature

Encourage others to respect and protect our wild spaces.

Outdoor ethics

To have adventures in the great outdoors is a privilege, but we have to protect our planet. Taking your rubbish with you, recycling, and avoiding single-use materials are great ways to protect the environment.

REDUCE

REUSE

RECYCLE

Organise a clean up party

Gather your nature-loving friends to join you in cleaning up your area. Make flyers to hand out so other volunteers can join in on the fun. You'll need to bring heavy-duty rubbish bags, work gloves, and a willingness to get stuck in!

Design your own flyer or copy this one.

Specify whether people will need to bring their own tools.

HOW TO BE A FRIEND TO NATURE

- Carry a reusable water bottle
- Keep all your belongings with you - leave nothing behind
- Bring a bag so you can pick up any litter you see along the way
- Avoid feeding or approaching wildlife

"Take nothing but memories, leave nothing but footprints."

Make seed cards

Send a message that grows.

You will need:

- ★ recyclable paper: newspaper, tissues, egg cartons, old letters
- ★ warm water
- ★ wildflower seeds
- ★ towels or cloths
- ★ large plastic container lid or parchment paper
- ★ sieve or strainer

Saving trees

Millions of hectares of forests are being destroyed every year to provide us with paper products. But recycling helps. Making plantable paper helps pollinators like bees and butterflies to do their work and keep our plantlife growing.

1

Gather together a pile of recyclable paper – this could be old letters, tissues, egg cartons, toilet roll tubes and newspaper.

2

Tear all your paper materials into tiny pieces and put them into a blender with some warm water. Use twice as much water as paper. Let it soak for an hour then blend until the mixture is pulpy.

3

Now sprinkle your wildflower seed mix into the pulp and stir it in.

4

Empty the pulp into a sieve and squeeze out as much water as possible.

TIP
Use a hairdryer on a cool setting to help speed up the drying process.

5

Place the pulp onto a sheet of parchment paper or a flat plastic container lid. Press the mix into a rectangular card shape, ensuring you spread it thinly and evenly.

6

Use a dry sponge, towel or cloth to soak up more moisture, then leave your seed card in a warm place to dry. Make sure you turn your card over to dry both sides.

7

When your seed card is completely dry you can decorate it and write a message.

Planting paper

As well as making amazing cards, you could make fun-shaped seed paper gift tags by pressing the pulp into cookie cutters. As well as a gift for your friends and family, you're giving a gift to the bees!

Find your way

Discover the meaning behind common trail marks.

Making a mark

On many hiking trails, it can be hard to know where you're going. To help others, people sometimes leave markers to help you 'read' a trail. This is called a blaze. A blaze was originally made by cutting a mark into a tree, but now there's lots of different ways of signposting a route, such as with paint, or by tying a ribbon round tree trunks.

Crafting clues

Set up trail markers for your friends to find you! You can use sticks, stones, grass, or draw marks in the earth to make your blazes. Take turns to set a route to follow – you could even place a prize at the end!

Tracking symbols

USE A SELECTION OF THE FOLLOWING TO MARK YOUR TRAIL...

	THIS WAY	TURN LEFT	TURN RIGHT
STICKS			
STONES			
LONG GRASS			

ANIMAL NAVIGATORS

Some animals are able to sense the Earth's magnetic field and use it to navigate. Pigeons, bees, sharks, and turtles all have these super wayfinding senses.

PACES TO A NOTE	DANGER	WRONG WAY	END OF TRAIL

Wilderness wishlist

Where in the world would you like to explore?

Use coloured pens or pencils to mark on the map where you'd like to explore. You could use one colour for places you've been, and another for places you'd like to go.

Write down any particular sights you'd love to see, or activities you want to do, like swimming with dolphins, or visiting the Grand Canyon.

Activities I'd like to try:

....

....

....

....

....

....

....

Be an aircraft engineer

Craft the best paper planes in the sky.

1

Fold the top right corner down to the left side of the page and open it up. Repeat on the other side.

2

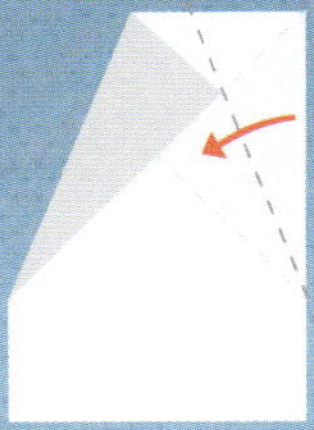

Take the left hand corner and lay it against the diagonal crease of the paper on the right side. Do this on the other side.

3

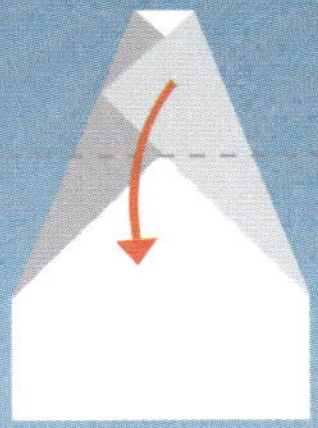

Fold the top down at the point where the two folds meet.

4

Fold both corners down along the creases. This will make a sharp point at the top – the nose of your plane.

5

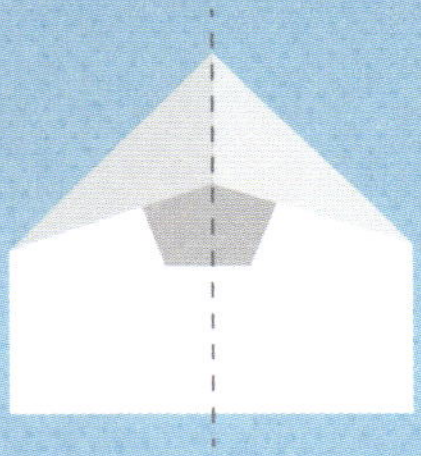

Turn the paper over and fold it down the middle (away from the creases), making sure to match the tail ends.

6

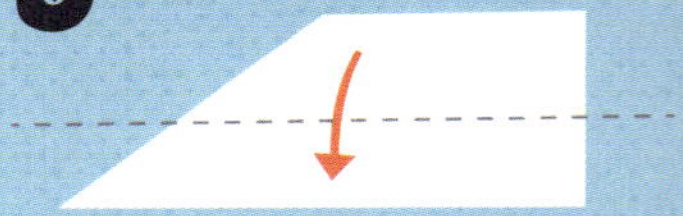

Roate the paper and fold the wing edge down. Fold the other wing to match.

7

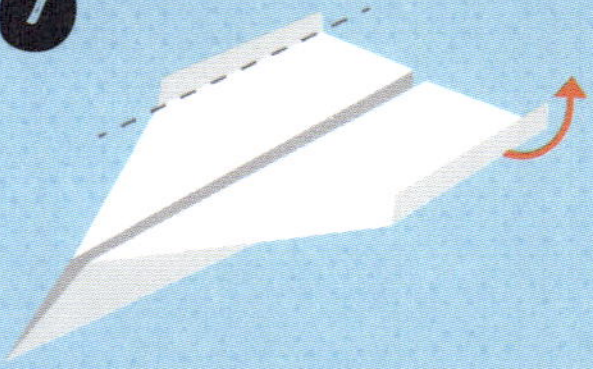

Open the wings up a little, and turn the corners of the wings up very slightly.

8

Hold under the nose of your plane, at the thickest point, and get ready for take off!

Different types of paper planes can loop, fly back to you, and even flap like a bat! Have a go at making these, too!

Talk like a pilot

The NATO phonetic alphabet was developed so letters had distinct names that were easily understood by everyone over poor quality radio channels. No one can get confused when you spell your name using the phonetic alphabet!

How do you spell your name using the NATO phonetic alphabet?'

NATO phonetic alphabet

Alfa
Bravo
Charlie
Delta
Echo
Foxtrot
Golf
Hotel
India
Juliett
Kilo
Lima
Mike
November
Oscar
Papa
Quebec
Romeo
Sierra
Tango
Uniform
Victor
Whiskey
Xray
Yankee
Zulu

Plane games

See how far your plane can glide for – have a tape measure at the ready. The world record for the longest ever paper aircraft flight is 69.14 metres!

Set up a large piece of card with different sized holes. Each hole is worth a different amount of points, the smallest hole is worth the most points. How many points can you and your friends score?

Grow your own veg

Learn how to grow your own salad.

You will need:

- ★ several pots or containers
- ★ bamboo canes
- ★ string or twine
- ★ potting soil
- ★ seed packets
- ★ toothpicks
- ★ card

From seed to salad

It's really fun and satisfying to eat food that you have grown yourself, and it's easy to do too! You don't even need a garden – food can be grown in pots indoors, or in window boxes, just as long as there's plenty of sunlight.

1

Fill a few containers with soil. These can be pots or even something like an empty ice cream tub.

2

Cut out labels for your plants from your card or paper. Write the name of your plant and tape the card to a toothpick. Push the toothpick into the soil.

3

Push the seeds about 2 cm into the soil, and about 3 cm apart from each other.

4

Place the container in a sunny spot. Water your plants every day or so and watch them grow!

Edible flowers

Some flowers are edible and provide the perfect finishing touches to a salad. Experiment by growing some of these tasty flowers!

Note: Never eat wild plants unless an expert or grown-up has told you they are safe.

Nasturtium

Pansy

Hibiscus

Dandelion

Marigold

Tomatoes

Start with small pots. When your seedlings grow around six leaves, move them into larger pots.

Put bamboo canes or stick into your pots for the plant to grow up. As it grows taller, gently tie the plant to the stick with string or twine.

Easy recipes

Have a go at these simple recipes that can be made using your own homegrown fruit and veg.

You will need:

- ★ tomatoes
- ★ shallots or onions
- ★ garlic
- ★ olive oil or butter
- ★ brown sugar
- ★ salt and pepper

Tomato sauce

Create the perfect sauce to pour over pasta, or smother on a pizza base.

1

Peel two shallots, or one small onion, and one clove of garilc. Chop them as small as you can. Watch your fingers – ask an adult to help you!

2

In a frying pan, heat a splash of olive oil, or a knob of butter on a medium heat. Add the chopped ingredients and stir for two or three minutes.

3

Optional extras: peppers, courgettes, fresh basil.

Harvest 300 g of ripe tomatoes from your tomato plant and roughly chop them.

4

Add the tomatoes to the frying pan, with a teaspoon of brown sugar and some salt and pepper to taste. Bring the sauce to the boil and cook for about 15 minutes. Add to a bowl of pasta for a tasty meal!

Strawberry smoothies

You will need:

- strawberries
- milk
- yoghurt
- optional banana and other fruit
- blender or food processor

Makes two smoothies

1

Pick around half a cup of strawberries from your crop, and rinse under cold water.

2

Add any other fruit at this point.

Put a couple of strawberries to one side for the garnish. Carefully slice the leafy tops of the strawberries with a knife.

3

Add the strawberries to a blender, along with 120 ml of milk and 170 ml of plain or flavoured yoghurt.

4

Cover and blend until smooth, before pouring the smoothie mix into two tall glasses. Slice partway into the two leftover strawberries, and push them onto the rim of the glass.

Pop a paper or metal straw into your drink and enjoy!

MAKE IT DAIRY-FREE

There are a bunch of dairy alternatives you can try. Check out coconut, oat, and almond milk. You can always add a banana to your smoothie for extra thickness.

Make discoveries

Keep your eyes and mind open – who knows what you might discover.

Be curious

Part of pursuing adventure means being open to trying new things, just to see what happens. Many discoveries come from trying to answer the question 'what would happen if...?'

Inspirational nature

Many inventions are prompted by nature. The first successful flying machines were gliders inspired by the wings of gliding birds, such as gulls. Velcro was inspired by an inventor on his walk, when noticing how burdock burrs stuck to the fur of his dog! Perhaps nature can inspire your next invention.

Close up of velcro hooks

ACCIDENTAL DISCOVERIES

Not all discoveries are purposeful. Sometimes they come about entirely by accident! In 1870, Thomas Adams was experimenting with South American tree sap, trying to make a substitute for rubber. He put the sap in his mouth and discovered he liked the taste, and just like that, chewing gum was invented. Check out these other accidental discoveries...

microwave

penicillin

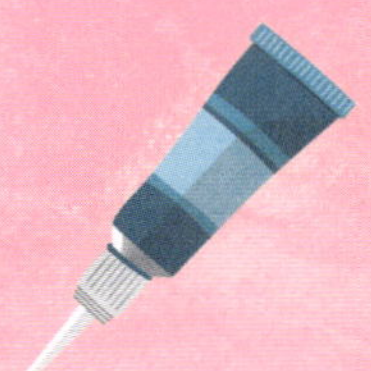

super glue

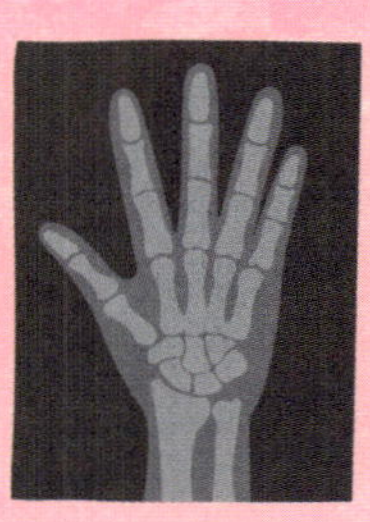

x-rays

Did you know?

There are tons of accidental discoveries that led to inventions we now could not do without, such as X-rays, microwaves, superglue and penicillin.

Growing experiment

Evidence

Experiment with growing bean plants (or another quick growing plant) in different light conditions. Does one grow quicker than the other? Does one grow better? Record your findings here.

The scientific method

- ☐ Make an observation
- ☐ Ask a question
- ☐ Set up an experiment
- ☐ Make a prediction
- ☐ Write down the results

"All life is an experiment. The more experiments you make, the better."

–Ralph Waldo Emerson

Space exploration

Humans have always looked up at the stars and wondered what's out there...

The final frontier

Astronomer Galileo Galilei was the first to turn a telescope on the night sky in 1610. Since then, people have strived to find out more and explore the farthest reaches of our Solar System.

Planet spotting

You don't need a fancy telescope to explore what's out there. Here's what you can see in the nightsky with a pair of binoculars and a helpful astronomy app or guidebook.

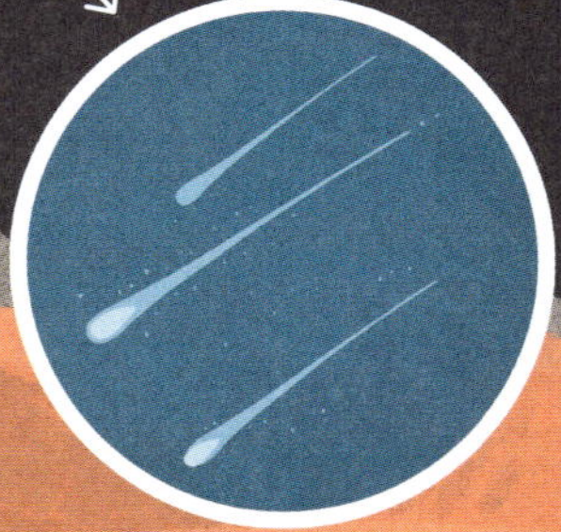

Party planet

Mercury orbits the Sun much faster than Earth. If you lived on Mercury, you'd have a birthday every three months. That's a lot of cake!

1957 – First mammal in space – Laika the dog

1961 – First human spaceflight – Yuri Gagarin

1969 – First humans on the Moon

ASTRONAUT TRAINING

Candidates have to undergo hours of intense training before they can be accepted as astronauts.

Can you tread water for 10 minutes?

Do you have what it takes?

- ☐ Good grades in science, engineering or maths
- ☐ A height of between 1.5 and 1.9 metres
- ☐ Good eyesight – 20/20 vision
- ☐ Good physical fitness
- ☐ Strong swimmer
- ☐ Survival skills
- ☐ Ability to be alone for long periods of time
- ☐ Ability to cope under pressure – both physical and psychological

The Red Planet

Space programs all over the world want to send people to Mars and create a permanent human settlement. Perhaps one day it will be as easy to get to Mars as getting on a plane.

What do you think will happen next?

1998 International Space Station built

2012 First probe in interstellar space – *Voyager 1!*

2030 *First humans on Mars?*

Assemble a survival kit

Put together a kit suitable for all emergencies.

TIP
Check the expiry dates on your survival kit items every six months, and replace them if they're out of date.

Keep items like a first aid kit near the top of your pack so they're easy to grab quickly.

Keep important things that you need to access easily in an outside pocket.

It's important to stay hydrated when out and about.

An emergency whistle can be heard over long distances.

Duct tape can be used to make repairs, help build a shelter, make a rope, or mark a trail.

Survival kit checklist

Tick off each item as you pack your bag. Use the space at the bottom to add any extra items.

- ☐ Whistle ....
- ☐ Headtorch / torch ....
- ☐ Batteries ....
- ☐ Glowsticks ....
- ☐ Waterproof bags ....
- ☐ Matches ....
- ☐ Energy bars / other emergency rations ...
- ☐ Reusable water bottle ....
- ☐ Compass ....
- ☐ Duct tape ....
- ☐ First aid kit ....
- ☐ Small knife ....
- ☐ Rain poncho ....
- ☐ Emergency blanket ....
- ☐ Sleeping bag ....
- ☐ Hand sanitiser ....
- ☐ Change of clothes ....
- ☐ Toothbrush and toothpaste ....
- ☐ ....
- ☐ ....
- ☐ ....
- ☐ ....

Be prepared

When outdoors, it's a good idea to carry a survival pack in case you get separated from your group. But this kit is also great to have on hand for other emergencies too, such as a natural disaster.

HOW TO PACK YOUR KIT

- Pack items such as matches and spare clothes in waterproof bags so they don't get wet or damaged.
- Check the weight of your bag as you pack – it shouldn't be too heavy to carry around with you.
- Arrange the heaviest items so they sit as close to your back as possible, between your shoulder blades.

Changing seasons

You might need to change items in your pack depending on the time of year. For example, add sun cream in summer, and warmer clothes and gloves in winter.

Survival skills

Discover survival tips that could save your life.

WARNING
Never drink from stagnant pools of water.

Collect water

Water is one of those most important requirements if you're stuck out in the wild. If you don't have a purifier, try one of these three methods for collecting fresh water.

Rainwater

Use a tarp, poncho, or plastic bag tied to tree branches to collect rainwater. If you hang it on a slant and place a container under it, the water can drain into it.

Transpiration

Tie a plastic bag to the leafy end of a plant, preferably one that's in full sunlight. Make sure there are no gaps for air to escape. Several hours later check on your bag – there should be some water that the leaves have released.

Dew

Use a clean cloths attached to your legs and go for an early morning walk through the plants. Wring out the cloths into a container, or directly into your mouth.

Check out page 26 for instructions on how to build a teepee style den...

...and page 52 to learn how to construct a hammock.

Build a shelter

Your first defence against the elements is a shelter. Choose a dry spot, preferably protected from the wind by trees, and try to line the ground with leaves to stop the cold rising.

Forest cocoon

Gather dry leaves, pine needles and bark and other forest debris into a pile that you can burrow into, like a natural sleeping bag.

Snow trench

1. Dig a trench in the snow big enough for you to lie down in, stomping the snow down to harden it.
2. Gather branches and sticks to lay across the trench, creating a roof, then cover the branches in foliage or tarp.
3. Crawl into your shelter. It won't take long for snow to cover the roof and provide shelter from the wind and the cold.

Survival mythbusting

Can you sort survival fact from fiction in this true or false quiz?

Circle your answer.

1	Drinking your own urine can keep you hydrated.	TRUE / FALSE
2	Head into the forest to avoid getting struck by lightning.	TRUE / FALSE
3	If a shark attacks you, punch it in the nose.	TRUE / FALSE
4	You can survive longer without food than you can without water.	TRUE / FALSE
5	In the jungle, you are more likely to be killed by a falling branch than a venomous snake.	TRUE / FALSE
6	You can suck the venom out of a snakebite.	TRUE / FALSE
7	Lie on your back to stop quicksand sucking you under.	TRUE / FALSE
8	Peeing on a jellyfish sting will relieve the pain.	TRUE / FALSE
9	Eat snow to stay hydrated.	TRUE / FALSE
10	You can lose up to five times more body heat if your clothing gets wet.	TRUE / FALSE
11	Birds flying in circles means a dead animal is near.	TRUE / FALSE
12	Dribbling can help you when trapped in an avalanche.	TRUE / FALSE
13	Stuffing your clothes with leaves can help keep you warm.	TRUE / FALSE
14	Tying a urine-soaked cloth around your head can help you keep cool.	TRUE / FALSE
15	Follow flying birds to find water.	TRUE / FALSE

Now flip the book to see how many you got right.

The results

1. False. There is water in urine. But there's also salt and urea, which are dehydrating. Don't drink it. Please.
2. True. Though nowhere outdoors is totally safe, it's best to be in a building.
3. False. Do you know how hard it is to hit things in water? If you can't put something between you and the shark, try attacking the eyes and gills.
4. True. You can survive roughly three weeks without food, but only around three days without water.
5. True. Don't forget to look up!
6. False. Trying to suck the venom out just adds bacteria to the wound, and venom to your mouth.
7. True. The worst thing to do is panic and flail around. Float on your back as close to the surface as possible, making small movements only.
8. False. Actually, this could make it worse. Painkillers are your best bet, or see a doctor if you're swimming in an area with particularly dangerous jellies.
9. False. Snow contains more cold air than frozen water and will lower your precious body heat. Always melt the snow before drinking it.
10. True. Get out of wet clothing as soon as possible.
11. False. Scavenger birds will swoop down if there is food available. Circling birds are riding the wamer air currents and likely still searching for food.
12. True. If you're trapped under snow, dribbling or peeing can help you find out which way is up.
13. True. Just make sure the leaves are dry first.
14. True. The wet cloth will keep you cooler. Shame about the smell.
15. False. While some birds like to spend time around water, others are just getting on with their lives. Don't trust that they're leading you anywhere.

My adventure goals

Document your goals and dreams for the future.

TIP
Set yourself a deadline for your goals - and stick to it!

Start small, dream big

We all have goals that can sometimes seem unattainable. To make them actually happen, you have to start small and break your goal into smaller steps. Remember that mistakes made along the way can help you learn, and that failure is a part of success.

Goal:

How do you plan to achieve this:

What obstacles do you need to overcome:

How will you do this:

Use this space to write down your dreams for the future, and what you can do to help yourself achieve them:

"A goal without a plan is just a wish."
–Antoine de Saint-Exupery

Discover

Use this space to write down experiments and record your observations.

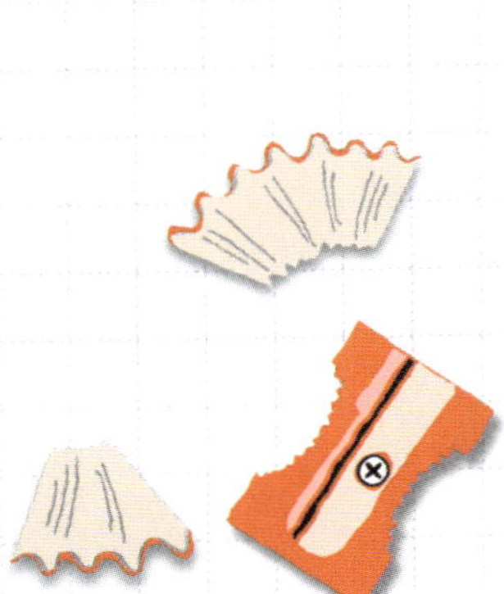

Create

Jot down ideas and stories here.

Design

Sketch, shade, doodle and draw.

Explore

Fill this page with artistic exploration.

Collect

Stick in leaves, feathers, and other small bits and pieces you can use to make a collage of nature.

Find out more

Check out these links online
to keep adventuring.

Help our wildlife
www.wildlifetrusts.org/actions

Mission X: Train Like an Astronaut
www.nasa.gov/tla

A knot a day
www.animatedknots.com/complete-knot-list

You should see this
thekidshouldseethis.com

Constellations and more
www.amnh.org/explore/ology/astronomy/a-kid-s-guide-to-stargazing

Song spotting
www.rspb.org.uk/birds-and-wildlife/bird-songs/what-bird-is-that

What is it?
butterfly-conservation.org/moths/identify-a-moth

Fossil finder
jurassiccoast.org/what-is-the-jurassic-coast/all-about-fossils/fossil-finder/fossil-finder-database